Stonehe

EARTH AND SKY

by

GERALD S. HAWKINS
and
HUBERT A. ALLEN, JR.

Stonehenge has been aptly named the Eighth Wonder of the Ancient World. Its story stretches from before the invention of writing to the advent of the computer and cyberspace. This book in the WESSEX SERIES *covers the story in broad perspective from the discoveries long-buried in the earth, to the inspiration of the sky.*

Contents

WESSEX BOOKS

What is Stonehenge?

A deep circular ditch and a low bank surround the monument.

The Stonehenge you see today is the crowning achievement of generations of ancient Britons living in the New Stone Age. More than 4,000 years old, the archways have stood as a bastion against time itself, and will continue to do so in the care of English Heritage as a World Heritage Site.

The archways at the centre are called *trilithons*, meaning three stones, two up and one across. The trilithons were ringed

around by thirty stones, joined together at the tops by flat lintels. Although they are more than 16 ft (5 m) up, a person could walk around on top of the lintels. The stones in this ring are called *sarsens*, but no one knows for sure where the name came from. Also the very name *Stonehenge* is a mystery – does it mean 'stones hanging in the air'?

From a distance the stones look jumbled, but from the air the neat pattern emerges. There were five trilithon archways set in a U-shaped design, and just inside this was a *Horseshoe* pattern of 19 bluestones from Wales. Between the trilithons and the outside sarsen circle was yet another circle of 59 or more bluestones. All of this lined up with an axis pointing to the midsummer sunrise on the longest day of the year.

The trilithons stand high inside the sarsen circle. At the top of the picture, Station Stone 91 lies fallen.

No small amount of construction work, and careful planning was needed to create this structure. Those people of the New Stone Age were the first to conceive of, and build, a free-standing stone archway.

Viewed from the air you can see the traces of the first Stonehenge, dug in the earth around 3000 BC. There was a deep circular ditch, 350 ft (107 m) in diameter, and 6 ft (2 m) deep, with a wide entrance at the north-east, and a smaller one at the south. This was not really dug into dirt or soil, but into the underlying chalk, a continuation of the White Cliffs of Dover. At that time the chalk fill was heaped up into a white wall, which would have been an impressive sight in 3,000 BC.

Even today, you can see the dip in the ground, and a slight rise where the ditch and chalk embankment stood.

Today's visitors use a walkway to view the giant stones.

In ancient times, a person could walk around the top of the lintels.

3

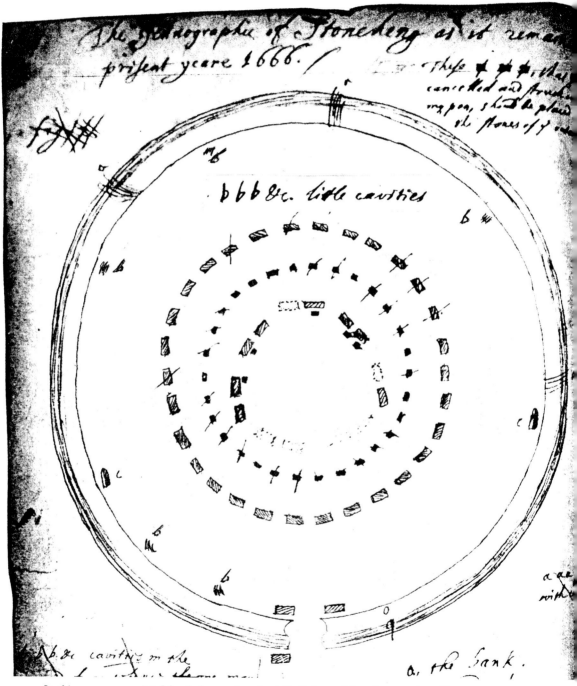

In this rare manuscript, John Aubrey writes about the little cavities *that now bear his name.*

An exact circle of 56 holes was placed inside the embankment with a diameter 284.8 ft (86.8 m). The holes ranged in British units from 3 to 6 feet across, and from 2 to 4 feet in depth. They were steep-sided and flat-bottomed, maybe for holding large posts, or wooden stumps.

Towards the end of the twentieth century the white chalk holes were covered with brown concrete making it difficult for visitors to see them in the grass. The Aubrey Holes should be made more visible; their regularity of spacing is impressive, and their still mysterious purpose an important part of Stonehenge.

They are called 'Aubrey Holes', and here there is no mystery about the name. In 1666, John Aubrey spotted tell-tale surface markings, and labelled them as little cavities on his somewhat inaccurate, but famous plan. In the twentieth century, some were still visible. An archaeologist, the late Richard Atkinson, said they showed up as raised frost domes during the severe winter of 1947, even though they had not been excavated.

The Heel Stone, a rough 35 ton boulder, was a focus for sun worship.

During the next few centuries a long Avenue was made reaching toward the sunrise from the north-east entrance. By this time the timber posts were long gone, and several stone patterns were made, only to be dismantled. The Heel Stone and its companion were placed to mark the centre strip of the Avenue, and four large stones were set in a rectangle on the circle of the Aubrey Holes.

Finally what could be called *Stonehenge Proper* was erected, with the monumental trilithons surrounded by the circle of huge sarsen stones. The last working at Stonehenge is not visible above ground. It came around 1700 BC when the Y and Z holes were dug, only to be left open to silt up with the wind and the rain.

What was the Purpose?

Ancient Britons were the first to use the free-standing stone archway – the trilithon. *Too narrow to walk through, was it meant to be looked through?*

The pomp is for both worlds, the living and the dead . . .
(Sir Walter Scott).

Unfortunately writing had not been invented in Britain during the Stonehenge period. It is difficult for us to comprehend what it was like to have no written record. The words and conversations disappeared in the air. The only clues we have are the stones themselves, the objects buried beneath the turf, and comparison with other cultures.

In use for perhaps a millennium and a half, Stonehenge was many things. When we accept one suggestion it does not mean that all other suggestions are wrong. It could have been a temple as well as a meeting place. It could have marked out past events, or be dedicated to the spirits of ancestors. Certainly its purpose was connected to and influenced by the sun, and the moon.

It seems that no crowds of people ever lived there. The earthworks covered as much area as ancient Troy, but no tell-tale foundations, pottery vessels or gold ornaments have been dug up. There was a period between the Aubrey Holes and the coming of the sarcens when post holes were sunk, and it is suggested that there was some sort of structure, but no habitation.

Religious worship was certainly involved. Stonehenge stands on a flat plain visible for miles around, resting between earth and sky. Places of worship have spires and towers reaching to the heavens, but Stonehenge brings the heavens to the people. In Neolithic times there was intensive agriculture and grazing, so the skyline was cleared of trees. The stones and archways seem to frame sacred points on the horizon.

Although it is called a henge, it is not like the hundreds of other ancient henges in Britain. By a quirk, these timber rings have come to be called in the twenty-first century by that name, even though there are no henge-like 'hanging' lintels. Perhaps the only connection is in the ceremony and religion, which Stonehenge brought to a climax.

Politically Stonehenge must have represented power within that long-forgotten society. Perhaps disputes were settled there, and decrees and laws proclaimed.

Certainly no major battles were fought on this hallowed ground, because archaeologists have found no shower of arrow-heads, no mass graves, no cache of stone weapons.

In the early stages the site was a burial place. Those posts did not stay in the Aubrey Holes for long. Year after year the chalk filling was lifted and replaced so that dozens of cremated remains could be buried there. Three skeletons have been excavated, but only one individual could actually be called a *Stonehenger*. After these early stages formal cremations ceased, and the powerful rulers of Wessex who came later had their burial mounds placed away from the sacred site.

Ceremony seemed to be important to the Neolithic people. There was a fine macehead, carved from a black and white stone at the site, and a venerated ox skull placed at the bottom of the ditch at the southern entrance.

Along with these political–social–religious suggestions must come recognition of the numbers chosen by the designers – numbers relating to the sun and moon. Significantly, other wooden henges in Britain do not show the number-system that Stonehenge does. Archaeologists suggest that the 56 Aubrey posts were used for attaching totem items, making it a recognised ritual number. It is also a number connected with the moon.

These two archways fell with a resounding crash in 1797, but were lifted up again with cranes and heavy equipment in 1958.

Some of the lintels weigh 7 tons, fashioned into shape with stone mauls, and seemingly 'Hanging in the Air'.

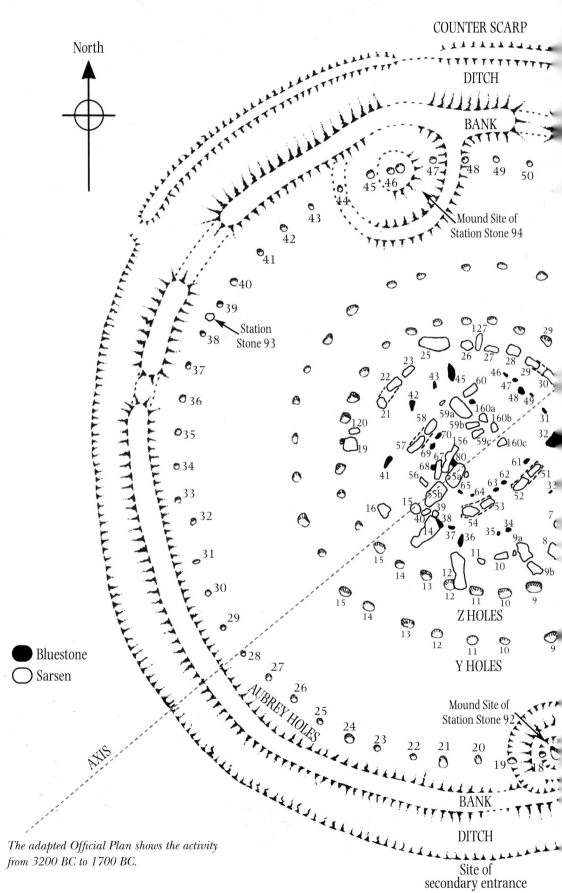

North

COUNTER SCARP

DITCH

BANK

47 48 49 50

45 46

44

Mound Site of
Station Stone 94

43

42

41

40

39

Station
Stone 93

38

37

36

35

34

33

32

31

30

29

28

27

26

25

24

23 22 21 20 19 18

Mound Site of
Station Stone 92

AUBREY HOLES

AXIS

● Bluestone
○ Sarsen

127

29

25 26 27 28 29

23 43 45 60 46 47 30

22 42 58 59a 160a 48 49 31

21 120 59b 160b 32

19 57 70 156 59c 160c

69 67 80 61

68 65a 62 51

56 65 63 52 33

55b 64 53 7

16 15 39 54 34

40 38 37 36 35 9a 8

14 11 10 9b

15 14 13 12 11 10 9

Z HOLES

Y HOLES

BANK

DITCH

Site of
secondary entrance

The adapted Official Plan shows the activity
from 3200 BC to 1700 BC.

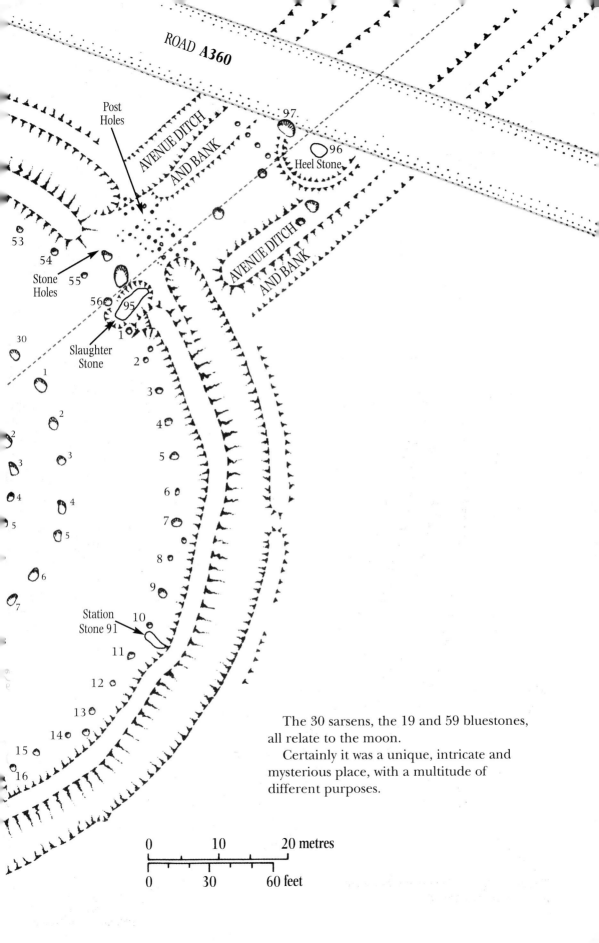

ROAD **A360**

Post
Holes

AVENUE DITCH
AND BANK

97.

96
Heel Stone

AVENUE DITCH
AND BANK

53

54

Stone 55
Holes

56 95

1

Slaughter
Stone

30

2

1

3

2

3

4

3

5

4

4

6

5

5

7

8

6

9

7

Station 10
Stone 91

11

12

13

14

15

16

The 30 sarsens, the 19 and 59 bluestones,
all relate to the moon.

Certainly it was a unique, intricate and
mysterious place, with a multitude of
different purposes.

0   10   20 metres

0   30   60 feet

How Old is Stonehenge?

As Stonehenge developed there was an axis of symmetry aligned with summer solstice sunrise and winter solstice sunset. Here the axis is viewed from the south-western end of the monument, looking to the northeast. Tallest and left of is the great trilithon Stone 56. The rounded-looking top of the Heel Stone can be seen just right of Stone 56, under a sarsen archway. The smaller 'finger' standing at right is a Bluestone.

If nothing has disturbed the layers, a sequence can be put together, with early things at the bottom, and later things at the top. That is how archaeologists knew the Stonehenge Avenue was made after the outer ditch had been dug. Sometimes the items can give a date, by comparison with other sites. But at Stonehenge the antique treasure trove was lacking. Only mundane objects like deer antler picks, a specially placed ox skull, and charred bone fragments of human cremations lay in wait to reveal the secrets of its age.

Here, the invention of radio-carbon dating gave the clues . . .

Carbon dioxide is drawn from the air to form the carbon in trees, plants, animals and human bones. The air is constantly bombarded by cosmic rays from the depths of space, making a portion of the carbon radioactive. It is only a slight effect, but by measuring the small amount left in wood or bone, the age can be found, because the amount gets smaller and smaller as the age increases.

Interpretation is sometimes difficult. An old antler could have been thrown in with later ones, or recent material could be accidentally mixed in with the old. The hard science is not as accurate as a clock ticking, but it is a useful clue.

The tall, thin Stone 56, the largest ever to be shaped in ancient Britain.

These large post holes, predate even the earliest phases of Stonehenge by thousands of years.

The first radio-carbon date we have is 7000 BC, give or take a few centuries. This was from charcoal in two large holes uncovered in the twentieth-century parking lot. It is far older than Stonehenge, and tends to be ignored. But the holes did once contain very large posts, and those posts were on the long line of the Station Stone rectangle. So it does show a human presence at the site.

But there is still room for debate on age. An individual date is uncertain by a few hundred years, so there is time overlap in the stages. For the Aubrey Holes there is a soil overlap which could put them back into the early period, if nothing has disturbed the layers.

Age Box	3200 BC	Bones found in ditch at south entrance
	2980 BC	Main ditch dug with deer antler picks
	2340 BC	Ditch filled or silted up
	2330 BC	Sarsen stones
	2270 BC	Human sacrifice near north-east entrance
	2230 BC	Avenue
	2120 BC	Bluestones
	1720 BC	Y and Z holes dug around the monument

The dates from charcoal, deer antlers and bones are given in the Age Box.

30 'Z' holes and 29 'Y' holes were dug and left to fill with the wind and the rain.

A section of the Aubrey Hole circle from the official plan.

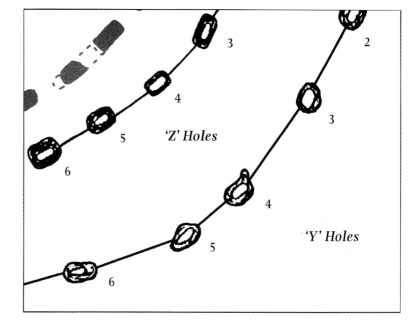

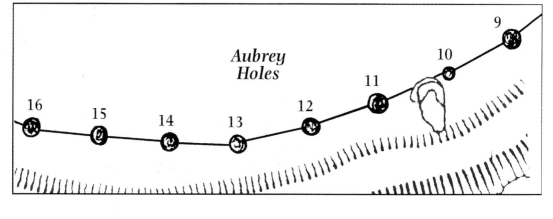

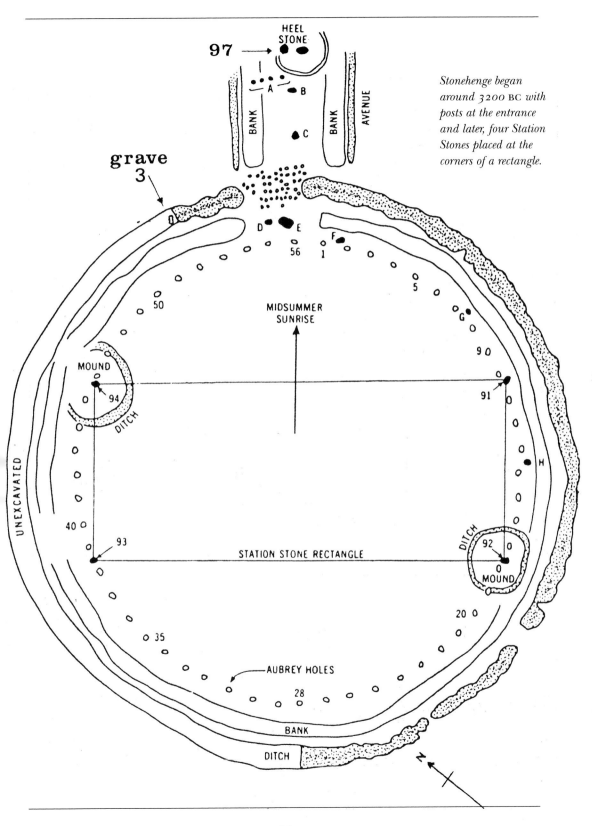

97

HEEL STONE

A   B

C

grave 3

BANK   BANK   AVENUE

D E
56   1   F

5

50

G

90

MIDSUMMER
SUNRISE

MOUND
94

91

DITCH

H

UNEXCAVATED

40

93

STATION STONE RECTANGLE

DITCH 92

MOUND

20

35

AUBREY HOLES

28

BANK

DITCH

N

*Stonehenge began
around 3200 BC with
posts at the entrance
and later, four Station
Stones placed at the
corners of a rectangle.*

Builders and Designers

Merlin

People used to believe the stones were set up by the magician Merlin. Others claimed visitors from outer space did it, but the evidence is for HTs (Human Terrestrials), not ETs. Today we would need computers and cranes, bulldozers and forklifts, but the Stonehengers had none of that. They were tough and determined in their purpose.

The sarsens are hard sandstone which came from the Marlborough Downs, 20 miles (35 km) north. The Ice Age left huge boulders when the glaciers retreated, and even now some lie half-buried in the ground. The sarsens were lifted out, and shaped by bashing with other large round stones called mauls.

The shaping work shows as unfinished grooves which were later smoothed down. Perhaps the long rectangular shape was helped in part by Mother Nature, and in part by heating and cracking the stone.

Without Merlin's magic, those huge rocks had to be dragged overland by men, women and oxen. (An ox is a cow or neutered bull.) One ox pulling equals five men. There is no wagon trail or wheel marks to show the way, but the route must have been across the Vale of Pewsey, and then by barge down the river Avon.

As though it were made of wood, the builders carved a tenon knob on the top of each sarsen upright.

The 5-ton Welsh bluestones must have been shipped by way of the treacherous Bristol Channel.

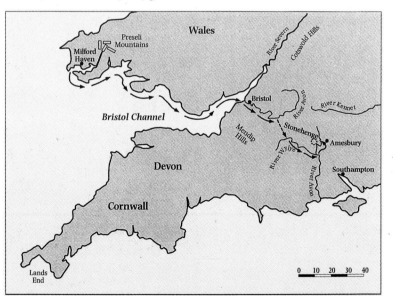

Some of the sarsen uprights weigh 50 tons, and stand from base to tip a formidable length of 25 ft (7.6 m).

Two mortise holes in the lintel fit neatly over the tenon knobs.

The 30 sarsens *(below)* make a ring accurate to within 4 inches (10 cm), and the tops are equally level.

Two small holes on top of the lintel *(right)* joining sarsens 30/1 line up with the sunrise axis.

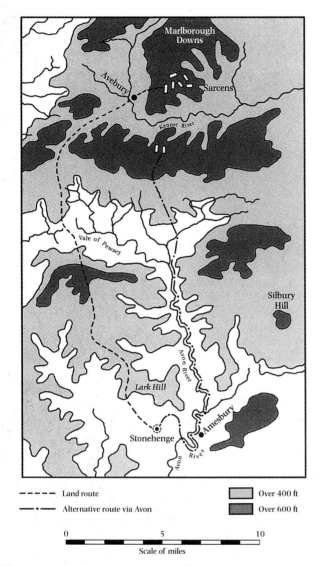

Land route

Alternative route via Avon

Over 400 ft

Over 600 ft

0   5   10

Scale of miles

The 50-ton sarsens may have been dragged overland, or else floated on barges down the River Avon.

The bluestones were smaller, with a weight of 5 tons, but the distance travelled to get them was ten times greater. They were on the steep side of the Preseli Hills in Wales. From here the ancient Britons took a sea passage along the Bristol Channel, with an overland stretch to reach and use the western river Avon. It is fanciful to call them Druids, because that cult got no official recognition until 1,500 years later.

At the site the stones were shaped as if they were wood. A carpenter making a doorway by hand would sometimes leave a knob of wood at the top, which fitted into a hole in the lintel for added strength. The knob is a mortise, and the hole is a tenon.

The knobs show on the uprights, and you can see the tenon holes on the fallen lintels.

This method of carving stone like wood is partly why Stonehenge stands today, surviving frost and weather, and the rare earthquake tremors.

Cutting the stones was very labour intensive, so if the sarcen was too tall, its hole was dug deeper to fit. The builders were already skilled in cutting wood, so we can imagine scaffolding, and levers at the site, and hundreds of people on the job. Each stone erected was an achievement calling for ceremony and celebration.

The 30 sarsens stand in a circle 94.3 ft (29.7 m) in diameter, accurate to a few inches. The inner faces of the stone are carved to fit this circle. The tops of the lintels are level even though the ground slopes downward to the north-east by 2 ft (60 cm). With designing finesse, the inner edge of each lintel is curved to fit the shape of the circle.

Thoughtful design also shows in the early Stonehenge, built by ancestors many generations before. The outer ditch has all the appearance of being a quarry for the chalk to make the embankment, but the Aubrey Circle is as exact as the sarsen ring. The number 56 divides by 4, so that 14 holes strike off 90°. The line from hole 56 to 28 marks the axis, later to be used in the final structure.

The Station Stones make a rectangle, and the short sides are parallel to the axis.

A strange mystery in the design was solved in 1979. The sunrise Heel Stone was offset to the right of the main axis. It is a 35-ton rough-shaped rock, leaning slightly toward the circle. We now know it had a companion on the other side of the axis to balance.

Each stone in the design has been given a number by archaeologists. The Heel Stone was the last to be labelled as No. 96, and the twin was therefore named '97'. Archaeologist Mike Pitts made the discovery only days before a telephone line was to be laid along the busy road, next to the old milestone and through a pile of buried Stonehenge debris.

The hole for stone 97 was discovered in this telephone trench in 1979. Note the Heel Stone 96 on the right.

The pyramids of Egypt can be compared with one another, and some had writing inside. But Stonehenge has no writing, and other henges named after it are so different they do not help much in our understanding of its design and purpose. Difficult though it is, we still try to reach back in time to those people of ancient Britain who lived and worked in what has become known as 'Hengeworld'.

Three Skeletons

During the first 500 years after the ditch was dug there were funerals and cremations at the site. Nothing much was left except a few small fragments of unburnt bone, which were collected and buried around the outer edge. Perhaps as many as 240 people were cremated. At a rate of one every two years they were not top leaders, but certainly were important enough to earn a Stonehenge resting place.

Some remains were at the bottom of the ditch, while others were deposited in the Aubrey Holes. With the 56 posts removed (if indeed posts had ever been there) the chalk fill was dug out, the cremation deposited, and the hole refilled.

After about 2,500 BC the favoured dead were no longer cremated and buried there, but for the living, surely the spirits of their ancestors lingered on.

Macabre though it is, a whole skeleton tells us more than a cremation, and three skeletons have been unearthed at Stonehenge.

Number 1 was buried on the axis, almost at the centre, and might have been a figure of importance. Unfortunately the skeleton is lost. It was held for safe-keeping in London, but apparently was destroyed in the bombing Blitz of the Second

Those burials that began whole history . . . under the wide Wiltshire sky . . . (Siegfried Sasson).

World War. The grave contained pottery, Roman coins and horseshoe nails, and no prehistoric evidence.

Number 2 was buried in a shallow grave in the flat area between the stones and the Aubrey holes. The man was an Anglo-Saxon, dating to 640 AD, and he was probably assassinated. Death was due to a swordcut at the back of the neck. At that period before good historic records there was much feuding between rival kingdoms in Wessex. A tragic story, but it throws no light on the people of 2000 BC.

There are other stray skeletons nearby in the area. One rich burial at Amesbury, a small town very close to Stonehenge, was identified by his teeth as coming from central Europe. What was he doing in ancient Britain around the time of Stonehenge – visiting, studying, worshipping? If indeed from central Europe, he adds to the greater mystery.

Number 3 in Stonehenge proper was buried near the original north-east entrance. This man had been a strong twenty-something, and had been ritually killed by three short-range arrows. He was buried head to the sunrise, no doubt as a sacrifice to the sun god. The radio-carbon date was 2270 BC, so those Yorick eyes in the skull had almost certainly gazed on a living Stonehenge. [Shakespeare refers to the skull of Yorick, the King's jester in *Hamlet* Act 5, Scene i.]

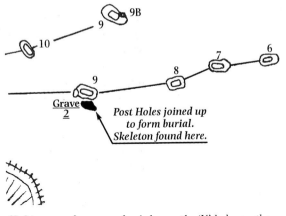

Skeleton number 2 was buried near the 'Y' holes on the official plan; archaeologists determined the bones were from a later Anglo-Saxon nobleman, executed in 640 AD.

Abandoned sarsen stones are said to lie beneath the waters of the Avon.

Grave 1, placed on the axis, held a mystery skeleton – was it Celtic, Roman or Neolithic? The evidence is obscure.

Grave 3, when Stonehenge stood in all its glory, this robust male was buried head-to-the-summer solstice sunrise near the entrance in 2270 BC. He was killed with arrows.

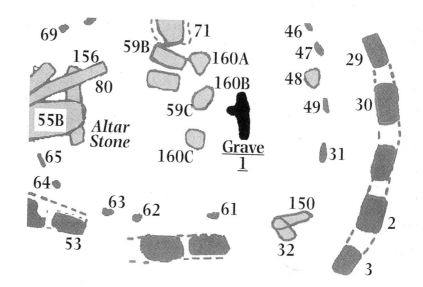

69
156
59B
71
46
47
29
80
160A
48
160B
49
30
55B   Altar Stone
59C
Grave 1
31
65
160C
150
64
63
62
61
32
2
53
3

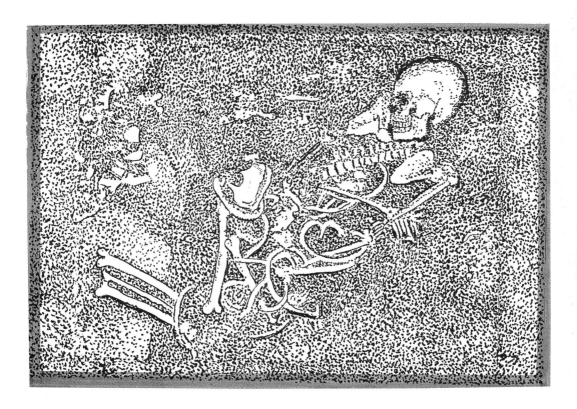

In the mid-twentieth century the 56 Aubrey Holes were marked clearly with white chalk-fill, as in the days of old.

The Station Stones

Before the archways went up, the central area was cleared and four rough sarsen boulders were placed around the edge. Numbered in sequence ahead of the Heel Stone they go from 91 to 94. Now called Station Stones, they were on the Aubrey Circle in a rectangle with diagonals crossing at the centre.

There were other stones, like E on the axis, and D placed to the left.

Numbers 92 and 94 have disappeared, but the holes show they were as large as the Heel Stone. Like that stone, they were sanctified with a special ring-ditch cut around them.

Who stole the stones? This is another mystery. It must have been heavy work to lift those tons, and carry them off. Maybe

. . . huge frame of giant-hands . . .
(Thomas Warton).

they are now part of some Wessex buildings. Salisbury cathedral is above suspicion, because in 1178 AD those 'Druid stones' were evil and damned. At Avebury, to the North, in medieval times, the stones were toppled over and buried, or cracked with fire and water.

They did not take away Number 91. It is 9 ft (2.7 m) long, and tilted outward. Number 93 is a low, smoothed stump, standing about 3 ft (1 m) high. The diagram on page 13 shows very clearly how stones 91 and 93 are placed in relation to the others.

Stonehenge as we see it now was built to neatly fit inside the rectangle, keeping the older lines of sight clear – which brings us to the design and purpose of the Avenue.

The Avenue

The Avenue is 45 ft (14 m) wide, with the centre line taken as the axis of the monument. The line runs between the Heel Stone and its twin, reaching out towards the midsummer sunrise.

There are three good reasons for the Avenue . . .

- It was a cleared strip for watching the sun and moon come up.

- It was a processional way for pilgrims to approach the monument at midwinter, when the golden sun was setting behind the archways.

- It was a track for dragging the heavy stones at the time the monument was built. After running straight for 1,600 ft (500 m), the Avenue turns to the east and drops down to the river Avon where the barges were unloaded. However, it would have been

There are many small holes at the Avenue entrance, which probably held posts to record the position of the moonrise as it changed from month to month and year to year.

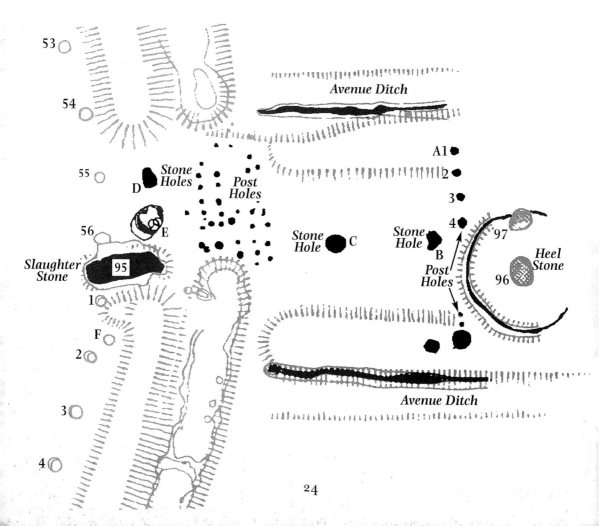

no easy task to drag those sarcens up that slope. Just imagine dozens of oxen, hundreds of men, all pulling on sledges, and lifting with long wooden levers. The hard work over the rough chalk earth was an achievement in itself to be proud of, whether or not it was done to please the gods in the sky.

The old entrance had pointed to the moonrise, but the new Avenue now shifted the entrance eastward towards the sun. The *Slaughter Stone* there is wrongly named – it originally stood upright next to stone E, and was not a flat slab for sacrifices. The many small holes probably held posts to mark the rising of the moon as seen from the centre.

Today civilisation moves fast, and the pace is quickening. We can hardly accept the idea of activities going on almost unchanged for hundreds of years, with inspiration and knowledge passed on by story, song and saga, from generation to generation. Yet that seems to have been the way of life in the Neolithic era.

The Slaughter Stone, 95, now lies flat across the north-east entrance.

Just before the sun has set, the moon can be seen as a pale disc over the stones.

On the summer solstice, in June, the sun rises in the Avenue and shines through the stones along the axis.

Midsummer Day

The distant Heel Stone, 96, and the archways make the famous stage-set for midsummer sunrise.

Thousands of modern-day visitors have witnessed the sunrise on Midsummer Day at Stonehenge. Astronomically it is the longest day of the year, summer solstice. On this day, people at the centre of the sarcen circle see the disc of the sun rising at its most north-easterly position, along the axis, just to the left of the Heel Stone. The tilt of the earth's axis changes slowly, so in 2300 BC the view was very much the same as today. The sun rose precisely on the axis between the Heel Stone and its now missing companion, Stone 97, and moved upwards in an arc until it stood on the tip of the Heel Stone.

The sun is so far away that it seems to move with you along the horizon as you walk from the centre out to the rectangle. That means that you see the same view of sunrise along the short sides of the rectangle, from Station Stone to Station Stone.

The observations box gives values for 2200 BC. Declination is like latitude on the earth's surface. It was 24° for the sun, and 29.1° for the moon back then. You can see how the offsets are all less than the width of the little finger held at arm's length!

Viewing Position (Stones and Avenue)	Observation of	Offset
91 seen from 92	Mid summer Sun	0.4°
94 seen from 93	Mid summer Sun	1.0°
Heel Stone–Centre	Mid summer Sun	0.0°
Avenue toward NE	Mid summer Sun	0.0°
93 seen from 94	Mid winter Sun	0.7°
92 seen from 91	Mid winter Sun	0.1°
Avenue toward SW	Mid winter Sun	0.4°
94 seen from 91	Mid winter Moon	0.4°
93 seen from 92	Mid winter Moon	0.6°

Naked eye observations by the Stonehenge people created alignments that were accurate to within 1 degree, an impressive feat in Neolithic times.

There are three lines for the sunrise, and there are also three for sunset. On the shortest day of the year at midwinter, the sun goes down opposite to its summer position. The rectangle now works in reverse with the sun setting over two low stones, and looking down the axis from the Heel Stone you see the archways stark against the sunset glow.

Modern day Druids celebrate the sun, but we can only imagine the ceremonies of the past. Those Stonehengers were not like the Druids of Celtic times; they celebrated the moon as well as the sun.

On Summer solstice a few minutes after sunrise, the sun has moved up and right to the top of the Heel Stone.

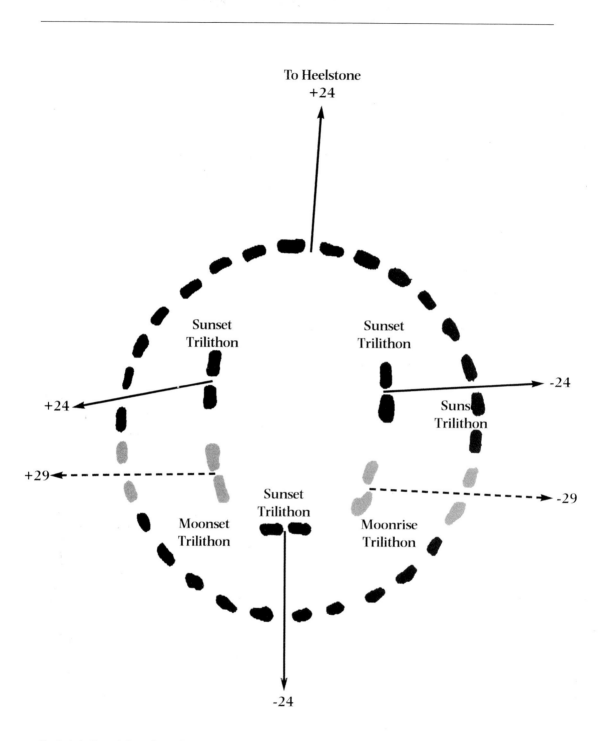

To Heelstone
+24

Sunset
Trilithon

Sunset
Trilithon

+24

-24

Suns
Trilithon

+29

-29

Sunset
Trilithon

Moonset
Trilithon

Moonrise
Trilithon

-24

In their hallowed days the archways framed the turnings of the sun and moon.

Midwinter and the Moon

In 1963, one of us (Gerald S. Hawkins) discovered how the moon and sun showed over the stones and through the archways at Stonehenge.

The Station Stones marked the moon on the longest moonlit night of the year. But not like the sun, those moonlit nights were longest in the special 'Year of the High Moon'. It rose then to the north-east of the entrance and set on the long sides of the rectangle.

Every month there was something to see at Stonehenge. In the 'High' year the moon was marked by rising over stone D. Month by month it changed from a crescent up to full. Then it set from full to the last crescent over stone 94.

Years of High Moon occurred at three intervals – 19, 18, and 19 – making the Stonehenge cycle of 56 years. At the midpoints of this cycle the winter moon took the place of the summer sun, rising over the Heel Stone. At that time it was in danger of eclipse.

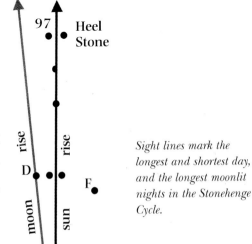

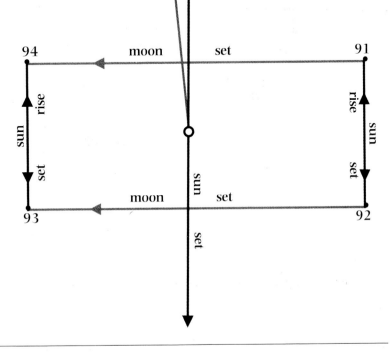

Sight lines mark the longest and shortest day, and the longest moonlit nights in the Stonehenge Cycle.

The sun at midwinter's eve as seen from the Heel Stone throws the monument into silhouette (see page 37).

Our research team witnessed this mid-cycle moonrise in December 2002. The photographs shown here take the reader back to the time when the Heel Stone was set up more than 4,000 years ago – back to that spectacular moment.

The trilithon archways are too narrow to walk through, so maybe they were meant to look through. The gap framed by the outer sarsens is about eight moon diameters wide, so the moon would certainly be visible there in the year of the High Moon.

The axis through the two trilithons at the handle of the horse-shoe runs parallel to the Station Stone rectangle. The nearest trilithon west could point to the setting of the full moon nearest to midwinter, and the trilithon further to the east the rising full moon nearest to Midsummer's Day.

High in the sky, the face of the moon shows through an archway..

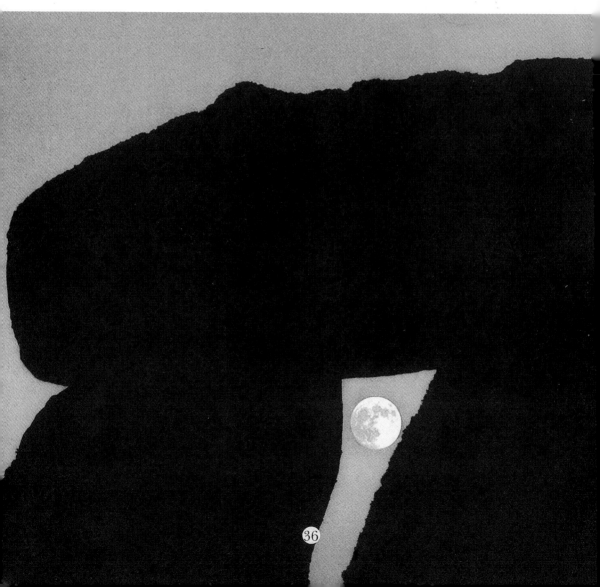

Accurate surveys could confirm this, and also whether the other three trilithons mark the sun. We know the great trilithon framed the setting sun at midwinter, and the one to the east-north-east even today shows the midwinter sun rising within its window. The west-north-west trilithon has fallen, but the holes in the ground show it was linked to midsummer sunset.

From the earliest times it seems as if the Stonehengers continued their observations of the sun and moon for more than 70 generations. Were these heavenly bodies gods to them? Did they control the seasons, agriculture and life, and even the spirits of life after death?

There is a cup-mark on lintel 29/30, perhaps to mark the nights of longest moonlight.

The full moon on midwinter's eve.

At the midpoints of the Stonehenge cycle the winter moon rises on the axis and moves up to the right at an angle of 32°.

Carvings and Numbers

The name chiselled on stone 53 is no mystery, it is of a seventeenth-century antiquarian who should have known better!

Lower down there is a hilted dagger, and a group of hafted axes, of Bronze or Stone Age. Since they are near ground level we assume the carvings were done after the stone was erected. But why? Perhaps they were symbols; perhaps memorials, or perhaps a set of astronomical numbers.

The axes and dagger carved here are genuine marks, but the name is not! It was carved for sordid glory by someone named De Ferre in the seventeenth century.

What about the hole on top of lintel 29/30? Was it a mistake, so the builder turned the lintel upside-down? Probably not, considering the care taken everywhere in the design. It could indeed have held a moon-marker.

Twentieth-century British archaeologists struggled with the astronomy at Stonehenge because of an overwhelming temptation to make it fit with other henges and because of the apparent intellectual sophistication implied by this astronomical knowledge. But Stonehenge is clearly exceptional. The numbers in the rings are numbers of the sun and moon. Stonehenge itself surely represents the apex of community achievement, learned over tens of centuries.

Consider the Aubrey Holes. The number 56 is the Stonehenge Cycle of 19, 18 and 19 years, when the sun and moon converge again over the starting marker stones. All the various moon phases and alignments could be counted off in this circle by using one hole per year. After 19, 18, and then 19 again, the grand cycle would be completed. The counting stone would be back at Aubrey Hole 1.

Calendar makers don't like the length of the moon-month. It is not a whole number of days; it averages out to $29^1/_2$. The Western calendar despairs of keeping in time with the phases of the moon. Other calendars that do observe the moon must alternate months of 29 and 30 days to keep in step with the first crescent.

The ancient Babylonians knew this fact, judging from the clay tablets, but was it found a thousand years before them in Britain? The 'Y' and 'Z' holes with 30 and 29 in each would have made an accurate pre-Babylonian day calendar.

As further recognition of the sequence of 29- and 30-day months, the number 59 was probably encoded in the bluestone circle. As the official plan shows, there is a bluestone in front of each sarsen, and also in front of each gap except for the entrance between 30 and 1. That adds up to the calendric 59.

What about the sarsen ring? There are not 30 complete sarsen uprights, only $29^1/_2$. Stone 11 in the sarsen ring was made half size. Surely the builders did not run out of stone – there was plenty more on the Marlborough Downs! It has been delib- erately carved and shaped to be the only half a stone. Is this stone half size because of the oddity of the moon-month? It would have been a remark- able achievement to know and represent the idea of half a day in half a stone.

Year of the High Moon

Yearly event markers

19y   19y

18y

Sarsen number 11, deliberately made half-size, stands in front of the trilithons. (It is known as 'shorty' by some archaeoastronomers!).

Sarsen 11, is now leaning. A Station Stone sits in the grass, and later-date Wessex burial mounds appear in the distance.

What the Ancient Greeks Said

There is no writing at Stonehenge in that period from 3000 BC to 1500 BC, and so we turn to later writings of the Greeks in the hope that their words tell us something connected with Stonehenge.

Diodorus of Sicily in the 1st century BC quotes other historians going back to 500 BC.

In the region beyond the land of the Celts there lies in the ocean an island no smaller than Sicily. This island . . . is situated in the north and is inhabited by the Hyperboreans, *who are called by that name because their home is beyond the point whence the north wind blows . . . Apollo is honoured among them above all gods . . . And there is also on the island a magnificent sacred precinct of Apollo and a notable temple which is adorned by many votive offerings and is spherical in shape.*

They also say how the moon, as viewed from this island, appears to be but a little distance from the earth . . . The account is also given that the god visits the island every 19 years, the period in which the return of the astron *to the same place in the heavens is accomplished . . . he both plays on the cithera and dances continuously the night through . . .*

Curiosity no longer falls entirely dead; some of the hundred questions have been answered ...
(John B. White).

44

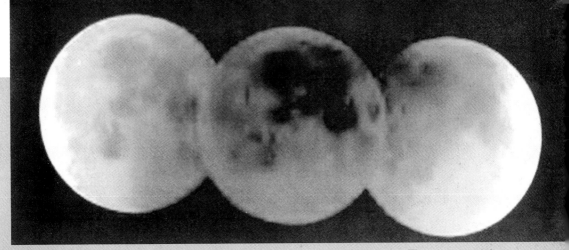

The word spherical might mean the celestial sphere. *Astron* means all luminous bodies. Actually, the sun, moon and stars return to the stone alignments not 19, but every 18 and $^2/_3$.years, in the Aubrey Hole cycle, 19–18–19.

Plutarch in the second century AD said that the Greek astronomer Eudoxus (350 BC) linked the number 56 with the god *Typhon*, or the *shadow of the earth into which . . . the moon falls and so suffers eclipse . . . which the sun remedies by instantly shining back upon the moon when it has escaped the shadow of the earth.*

Again we have a connection with the Aubrey Holes, and also lunar eclipses. At midwinter's day, the earth's shadow (Typhon) lay behind the Heel Stone, and if the full moon in mid-cycle arose at that spot, then it was eclipsed.

The moon moves into Typhon, the deep red shadow of the earth, and through eclipse phases in this time-lapse photograph.

Stonehenge in 3000 BC was a bold and grand endeavour to join earth and sky, to lock the patterns of the sun and moon in post, stones and archways. Even when the work was ended around 1700 BC its fame continued to be recognised far afield, across the ages of time, into the present day.

Further Reading

'Stonehenge and its Landscape', 1995, Cleal and others, London, *English Heritage Report* Number 10.

'Some New Measurements on Stonehenge', 1978, R.J.C. Atkinson, *Nature*, London, Volume 275, page 50.

'Stonehenge Decoded', 1963, G.S. Hawkins, *Nature*, London, Volume 200, page 306.

Astronomy in Prehistoric Britain and Ireland, Clive Ruggles (Yale University Press), 1999.

Beyond Stonehenge, Gerald S. Hawkins (Hubert Allen and Associates), 2000.

Hengeworld, Mike Pitts (Arrow Books), 2001.

Stonehenge Decoded – New Discoveries, Gerald S. Hawkins (Hubert Allen and Associates), 2003

Acknowledgements

For the use of photographs and artwork not supplied by Gerald S. Hawkins, the publishers gratefully thank:

Hubert A. Allen Jr p.19, bottom;

Ashmolean Museum, p.4;

Joeff Davis, front cover, pp.3 top, 6 bottom, 18, 22, 26, 30, 34, 36, 38, 42, 43, 46, back cover;

Fred Espenak, p.45;

Pete and Alison Glastonbury, p.38;

Ministry of Public Buildings and Works, England pp.8, 21;

Lucy Pringle, p.2 bottom.

Cover illustration by Andrew Jamieson

Designed and edited by Jane Drake

Published by Wessex Books 2004

Reprinted 2006, 2009, 2013, 2015.

Text © Gerald S. Hawkins and Hubert A. Allen Jr

Design © Wessex Books 2004

Typesetting by Wessex Books

Computer-aided map work by Alexander S. Grenfell

Printed in India

ISBN 978-1-903035-24-5